CRAFT MANUAL
of
NORTH AMERICAN
INDIAN
FOOTWEAR

by

GEORGE M. WHITE

ILLUSTRATIONS AND DRAWINGS
BY THE AUTHOR

George M. White is also author and publisher of:

"CRAFT MANUAL OF NORTHWEST INDIAN BEADING"

"CRAFT MANUAL OF YUKON TLINGIT"

"CRAFT MANUAL OF ALASKAN ESKIMO"

"WINDSHIELD GEOLOGY OF THE FLATHEAD"

"LIVING IN MONTANA"

Publisher of

"AN OLD INDIAN TOLD ME, BY GUMMY", By Dave Harriman

"TELL ME, AHNA", Eskimo Folktales, by Susan Towne DeBree

G-6   Page 14

Fig 61
Page 48

Fig. 58   Page 47

Fig. 66
Page 52

Fig.70   Page 58

Fig 73
Page 60

Fig 77   Page 54

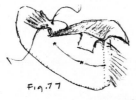

Fig.77
Page 54

Fig. 20

Page 24

Fig. 22   Page 30

Fig. 9   Page 20

Fig. 25   Page 31

Fig. 13   Page 22

Fig. 28   Page 32

Fig. 18   Page 28

Fig. 3   Page 27

Fig. 31   Page 33

Fig. 44   Page 38

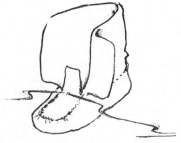

Fig. 35   Page 34

Fig. 46   Page 40

Fig. 39   Page 36

Fig. 49   Page 42

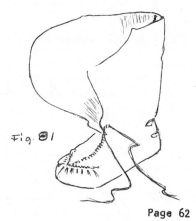

Fig. 81

Page 62

Fig. 53   Page 44

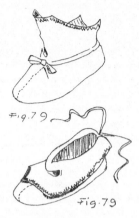

Fig. 79

Fig. 79

Page 56

INTRODUCTION

The word Moccasin just happened because the Algonquin people along the New England coast told the first white settlers the name of their footwear. The word has since been used to identify the leather footwear of most of the Indian people in North America.

Most of the Moccasins were made of soft tanned leather; there are some exceptions, but for the most part the tanning process was basically the same with all peoples. The fleshing (removing all tissue, fats and flesh on the inside of the hide) was necessary in all cases. Hair was removed or left on, depending on its intended use. If hair was to be removed, the standard method was to chop or scrape the hair off. This method always removed the outer "grain" of the leather, producing the suede look of all Indian tanned leather. Various methods were used to "break down" and soften the leather. One ingredient was always there and that was hard manual labor. The soften leather was white and often left that way by some Plains people, but for the most part it seems all woodland people preferred to smoke their leather as this aided in the tanning and service of the leather. The smoking produced a brownish leather which withstood moisture better than the white leather.

Moccasins were found in all North America except south of the border in Mexico and the northern fringe where Eskimo cultures prevail. This is, of course, only a broad statement with exceptions.

As we study Moccasins several points of interest appear. We might become curious about distribution of a particular type or why a certain type is found in a certain location, or we might wonder as to how long it took to perfect the footwear we see today.

As for time, the archeologist an other specialists tell us that it would have been possible for early man to have made a footwear seventy-five thousand years ago. The last Great Ice Age would have forced many northern hunters to perfect a protective covering for his body. The Ice Age may have caused people to migrate onto the North American Continent. It is fairly well agreed that man has been on this continent twenty-thousand years. The remains of his culture are comparable to the culture of Europe of the same period. The remains are necessarily stone implements as organic materials have small chance of surviving so great a time.

There are at least two reasons why we think this early North American had a footwear. First, the stone artifacts of his culture indicate he was intelligent enough to produce leather goods. Secondly, if he had come to this land by the northern route, from Asia to Alaska, then it would seem most necessary that he had some protection for his body and feet.

Twenty-thousand years ago the Great Continental Glacier must have sprawled over the entire land mass of Canada and pushed into the United States. Thousands of Alpine Glaciers spewed ice and frigid waters into mountain valleys from Alaska to California. There may have been ice free corridors running north and south that would provide passage as well as plants and animals for food.

The distribution of Moccasin types also offers food for thought. We assume that we have twenty-thousand years to consider distribution and movement of people and also the same time for perfection of design. We must consider some limitation as to ways leather can be manipulated to produce a footwear. The "Center Seam" as a basic design seems to have the greatest distribution and is the most predominant design. The "Gathered Toe", "Side Seam", "Two Piece", (hard sole and soft sole), and "Shaped Sole" fall into smaller areas of less distribution.

The distribution seems to indicate a possible inter-play of cultures and people in an arc south of the Great Lakes to Maine and perhaps a long the southern fringe of the ice mass.

A series of designs show up in this area while north of this line a predominant type (a modified center seam) moves north to the Arctic following the retreat of the ice. South of this line a true center seam prevails. In a Southwest section joining this line, a third modified center seam (see Winnebago) is found. Closely related in the same area is found a side seam type which also appears in the Western Rocky Mountain areas.

The "Two-Piece" hard sole appears (as a modification) on the high, dry Plains in the west. Several things indicate that this "Hard Sole" Moccasin was a product of the high Plains as a must rather than a choice. The hard sole was harder to make than the soft sole, but it gave greater protection from cactus and hard prairie ground.

The last Moccasin to be considered is the Apache and Navajo. We are told that these people were the last group to move down from the north. The Moccasin study also indicates this as there is strong resemblance in design of the Apache, Navajo footwear to the Northern Indian and Eskimo Mukluk. This Moccasin group will be called the "Shaped Sole" type. It would seem to suggest that these people moved from the north rather quickly and retained their footwear designs and found them as well suited to the harsh desert and plains as they were to northern ice.

The Apache also retained an odd shaped sole design that has distinct "Mongolian" characteristics. The lifted, pointed toes is also suggestive of Lapp footwear.

Many North American Indian Moccasins show characteristics of Asian footwear, but as mentioned before there are limited ways in which leather can be manipulated and it is possible many different groups could have developed similar designs.

The time element and designs development can only be projected from bits of information and close examination and study of Moccasins. This examination reveals a degree of perfection, considering the use of leather, tools and materials available, and the final product. This we choose to call "Climax Design", where there is little or no way to improve a particular Moccasin's construction. Most Moccasins show this "Climax Design", which must not be confused with transitional or "break-down" periods when the Indian economy was disrupted or destroyed by European advances.

Bits of information such as nine thousand year old sandals show sophistication and skill of that time; the needle of bone, dated thirteen thousand years; the Julian Steward Moccasin Collection dated eighth hundred to nine hundred years ago, revealing "Climax Designs" equal or superior to a comparable Moccasin found in the Yukon today. These tend to indicate the age of Moccasin designs. The designs shown in this book could be from one thousand to ten thousand years old. The center seam type might even be older that ten thousand years.

The main types are shown in this book. There are many variations of these types which are not illustrated.

GENERAL INSTRUCTIONS
for making moccasins

The following instructions should be used for the laying out and making all of the moccasin designs in this booklet. Special instruction will be found with each pattern. Heel and tongue detail sheets illustrate particular methods of handling. A sheet of stitches shows stitches found in old-time moccasins. It is recommended that the novice use the simple "whip stitch" before attempting some of the more complicated stitches.

The following steps should be observed for laying out all moccasins, unless a precut kit is used.

1. Place a large piece of paper on the floor.
2. Place either foot on the paper. (see drawing G-1)
3. Hold pencil perpendicular and trace foot outline.
4. Draw in line **L M** as shown in figure G-2.
5. (For a foot that is longer than 9 inches, add 3/4" to heel and 1/2" to the toe.)
6. Mark these measurements on paper on line **L M**. (These may vary with design.)
7. Draw line **A B** as shown in Figure G-2 and G-3. Use string and measure circumference of foot at this point.
8. Mark this measurement on line **A B**. Double the string and place loop end on the center line **L M**. The other end should give location of **A** or **B**.
9. **L M** and **A B** are needed for all moccasins to produce a good fit.
10. Turn to the moccasin design to be copied and make your pattern of the foot tracing. Note the special instructions.
11. If heavy leather is used add 1/4" to pattern along **A B** measurements to allow for seams.
12. After laying out the pattern on paper and rechecking measurements cut out the pattern. Do not cut out any tongue drawn on pattern in dotted line.
13. Lay leather out on a large surface such as a table top. Place the paper pattern on the leather as shown in G-4. (Position pattern parallel to or at right angle to the back line, never on a bias.)
14. When the design calls for a left and right pattern, use the same pattern but be certain to turn the pattern over before tracing the second pattern on the leather.
15. Lay pattern against the edges of the leather- to save leather- and trace the second piece as close as possible for the same reason.
16. Be sure to check leather under pattern for cuts, thin spots, or holes before tracing the pattern. (Ballpoint pen marks cannot be removed except by cutting off.)
17. Trace all patterns as close together as possible and cut out.
18. Special instructions should be noted at this point.
19. Sewing is started at the toe after centering at point **M** and going to the heel. This allows the novice to make adjustments at heel. Be sure to tie off beginning the end of each thread.
20. Special sewing instructions are found with each drawing.
21. All soft soled or woodland type moccasins are made snug as they loosen with wearing. The hard sole and the shaped sole moccasin are made a bit larger because the sole piece will have less give and stretch than the soft sole type.
22. Tie Strings - See Figure #5. Tie strings are cut from scrap leather 4" or 5" in diameter. DO NOT USE flank leather as it is weak and stretches. Cut string about 3/8" wide and about 36" long. Test by stretching before using. Note special instructions for attaching tie strings for each design. See tongue detail sheet.
23. Holes for tie strings are never cut. Always make holes with an awl or a pointed tool.

Figure G-5 to G-8 illustrate the relationship between sole and vamp-upper piece or sole and insert.
Figure G-5 shows both sole and vamp being the same width and together the two pieces equal the circumference of foot at line **A B**.
Figure G-7 shows sole the same size as foot tracing and the vamp must be wider to complete the circumference.
Figure G-8 shows sole (e.g. Yukon Type) much wider than foot outline and the insert completes the circumference. With all these measurements 1/4" should be added to allow for seams which take away from circumference measurements.

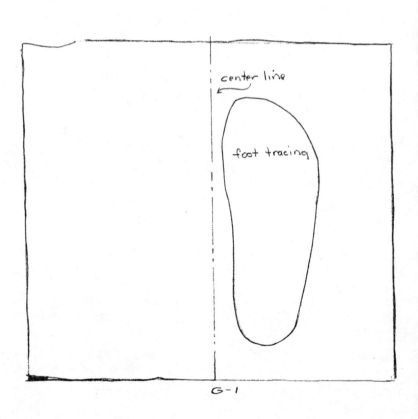

center line

foot tracing

G - 1

GENERAL INFORMATION
For all Leather Footwear

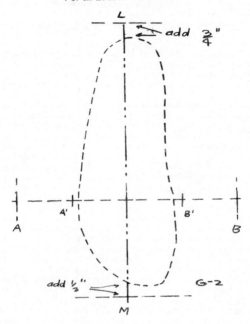

A B = Largest c̲ircumference of the foot at this point. This measurement must be co̲n̲sidered in all designs to obtain the proper fit.

A' B' will vary with pattern, but is always less than **A B**.

L M = Length measurement of leather. This measurement all vary with different designs.

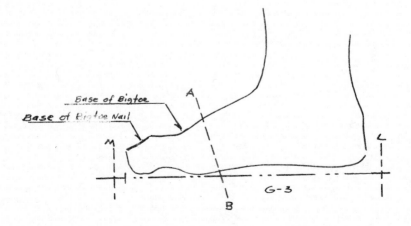

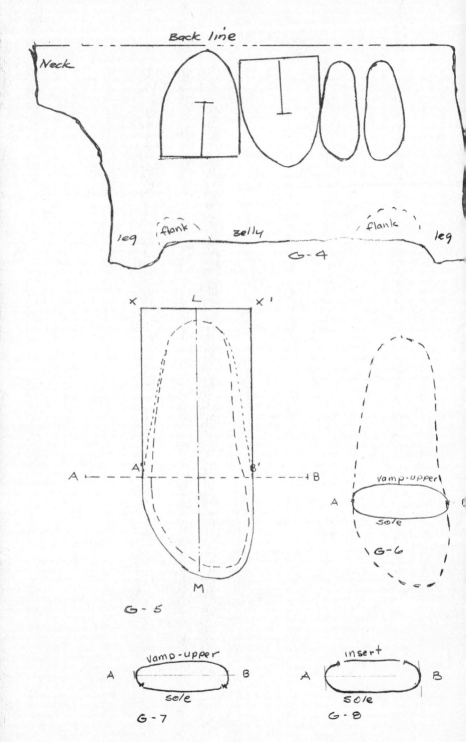

Back line

Neck

leg   flank   Belly   flank   leg

G-4

X   L   X'

A — A' — — — B' — B

M

G-5

Vamp-upper

A   sole   B

G-6

Vamp-upper

A   sole   B

G-7

insert

A   sole   B

G-8

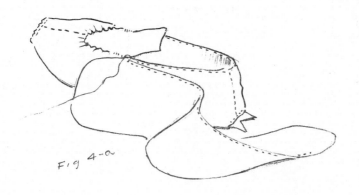

Fig 4-a

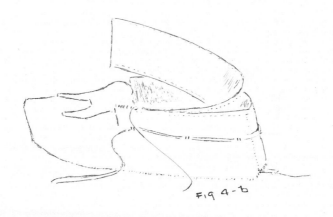

Fig 4-b

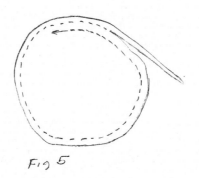

Fig 5

Tongue and tie-string Details

Heel details

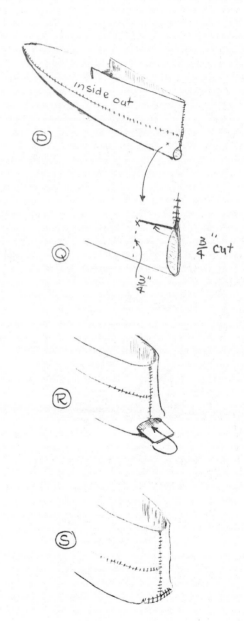

inside out

$\frac{3}{4}''$ cut

$\frac{3}{4}''$

sewing parfleche soles

flesh side

sole

grain side

(G) Angle of attach of
needle or awl

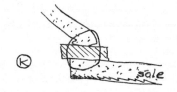

(K)

sole

upper

sole

(H) whip stitch

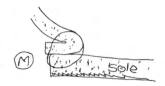

(L) upper

sole

(I)

sole

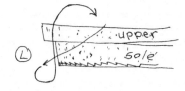

(M) sole

(J) upper

WELT

sole

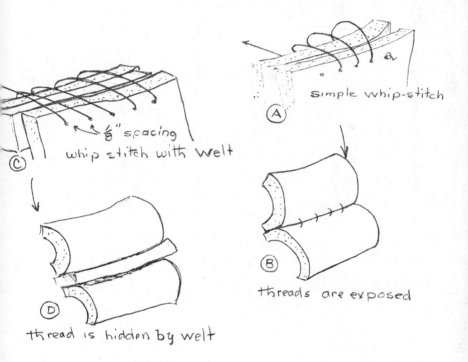

simple whip-stitch

(A)

(C) ←⅛" spacing
whip stitch with welt

(B) threads are exposed

(D) thread is hidden by welt

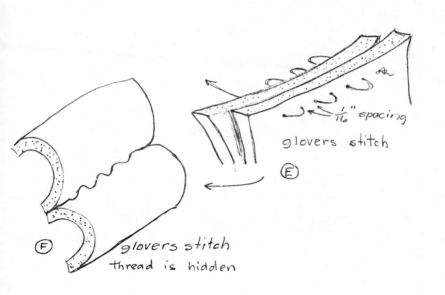

←1/16" spacing
glovers stitch

(E)

(F) glovers stitch
thread is hidden

IROQUOIS "CENTER SEAM"

1. Trace outline of foot.
2. Measure **A B** (see General Instructions on page 11)
3. Measure **L M** (allow 3/4" at heel and about 1 1/2" beyond the big toe, or, allow enough material to cover the heel and lap the big toe completely.
4. Place these measurements on foot tracing.
5. **C X** measure is found by adding 3/4" at heel and 1/2" at toe of foot tracing.
6. Point **A** is 1/2 the distance of **C X** .
7. Line **A B** is circumference of foot.
8. **A'B'** plus tongue-insert piece is equal to **A B**.
9. Angle between **H K** and **H'K'** is between 100 -120 degrees. Figure 6.
10. The arc between **K** and **K'** is about 1/2 the distance between **A'** and **B'**.
11. Fold the paper on line **L M** and cut pattern so both sides will be symmetrical.
12. Do not cut out the tongue pattern. See step 22.
13. Make 2 tracings of pattern on leather and cut. (CAUTION. See General Instructions for placing pattern on leather, page 11 #13 and page 14 G-4.
14. There is no left or right foot to this design.
15. Sew by folding leather inside out. Bring **H** and **H'** together. See Fig. 8.
16. Use 1/8" whip stitch on all seams, except where gathering is necessary.
17. Sew **H H'** to **K K'**. Fig. 8.
18. Turn moccasin right side out. Bring center of toe flap to point **K K'**.
19. Close toe with a gathering stitch: 1/8" stitch on short run and 1/4" stitch on long run (**M**). See Fig. 8. Tie off each end of thread.
21. Sew heel next. Turn moccasin inside out . Bring **X X'** together. Sew down to heel cut using 1/8" whip stitch. Turn moccasin right side out.
22. Cut tongue out next. Make tongue pattern as shown in Figure 6. Determine tongue width so that **A' B'** plus tongue equal **A B** (circumference).
23. Sew tongue to moccasin at point **A'** where the tongue piece begins to taper. Use gathering stitch: 1/4" stitch on moccasin piece and 1/8" stitch on tongue.
24. The foot opening should be 1/2 the length of the moccasin.
25. Turn heel tab up and catch with a few stitches.
26. Top extensions are added. (See Fig. 4-a, page 15)

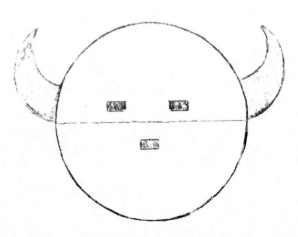

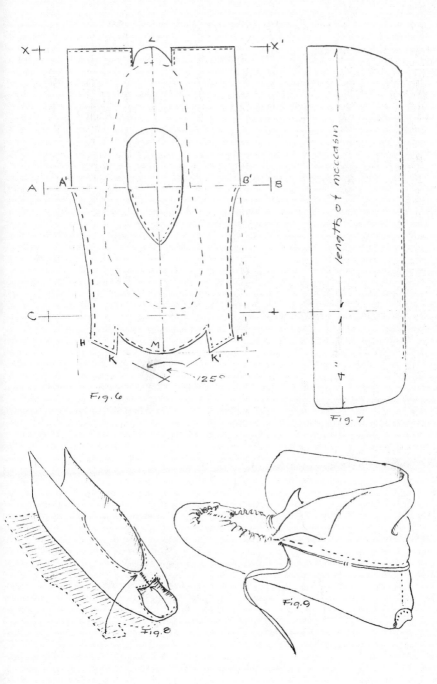

X
X'
L
A | A'
B' | B
C
H
K
M
K'
H'
125°
Fig. 6

length of moccasin
4"
Fig. 7

Fig. 8

Fig. 9

-21-

YELLOW KNIVES - "CENTER SEAM"

1. See General Instructions.
2. Special instructions as follows:
3. Line **L M** = (length of foot + 3/4" at heel + 1/2" at toe)
4. **A B** measures circumference.
5. **A' B'** measures leather which added to tongue insert is equal to **A B** or
   (**A A'** = 1/2 width of tongue.)
6. **O K** = 1/2 **H K**
7. Make pattern: trace foot, draw all measurements on pattern.
8. Fold pattern on line **L M** and cut both sides symmetrical.
9. Trace pattern on leather. (See general instructions for tracing on leather.)
   Cut two leather patterns alike as there is no right or left.)
10. Fold leather inside out.
11. Sewing: join **H H'** and sew to **K K'**. Use 1/8" stitching.
12. Sew toe with 1/8" stitch and turn outside out.
13. Cut out tongue piece. (See Fig. 12 for shape.) Width of tongue should be equal
    to **A B** when added to **A' B'**. Length where stitched to moccasin is about 1/4
    length of foot tracing.
14. Center tongue as it appears in Fig. 10. Start sewing at **H H'** (see Fig. 14)
    Use 1/8" stitch on the tongue and 1/4" stitch on side piece as sides must be
    gathered. Sew to **B'** tie off and sew second half of tongue.
15. Sew heel either inside out or right side out. (See heel detail on page 17.)
16. Cut out and sew on extensions. (See Fig. 4-a, 4-b on page 15.)
17. Tie strings and extensions. (See page 26, numbers 23 -27.)

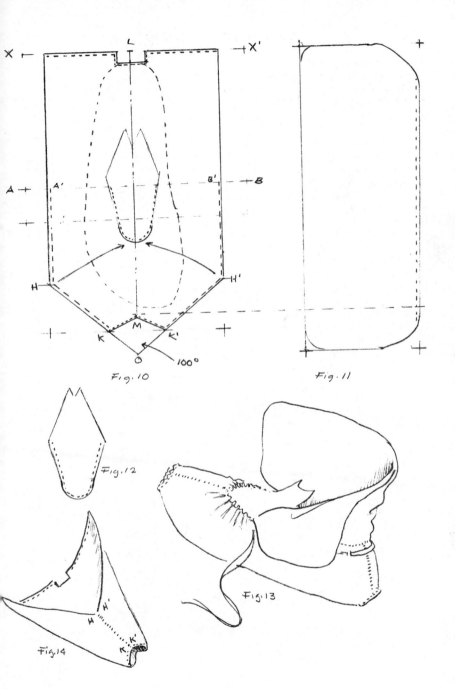

X ⊦ L +X'

A + A' B' + B

H H'

M K'
K
O 100°

Fig. 10

Fig. 11

Fig. 12

Fig. 13

Fig. 14
H H'
K K'

-23-

POINT TOE - SIMPLE CENTER SEAM

1. See General Instructions.
2. **A B** is full circumference.
3. **L M** is (for average 9 to 12 inch foot size) length of foot plus 1/4".
4. Note there is no heel cut.
5. Sewing: Fold on line **L M**, inside out.
6. Sew from **M** to **A B** to about one inch from flaps; tie off thread securely.
7. Sew heel from **X X'** to **L**.
8. Turn moccasin right side out.
9. Sew second moccasin in same manner.
10. Note the 3 foot outlines in Fig. 19. The left and right tracings are
    more important positions as they will show the amount of leather needed
    to cover the foot.

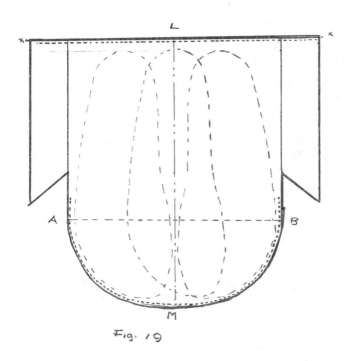

Fig. 19

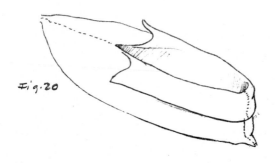

Fig. 20

KOOTENAI "CENTER SEAM"

1. See Fig. 1 for general design.
2. **A B** line is the circumference line and must include the tongue insert and the sole piece. (Note change in position of line **A' B'**.)
3. The length of the sole piece can be determined by measuring **L M** line; allow 3/4" at heel and measure under big toe and over to base of big toe nail. (See Fig. G-3)
4. Determine curve at **M** by dividing width in three parts. (See Fig. 1.)
5. The depth is found on line **L M** and intersection of line **C**. This point is on **L M**. (3/4" at heel + length of foot tracing + 1/2" at toe.) This also gives point **A'** which is midway between **X** and **C**.
6. **H K** and **H' K'** are set at a 100 degree angle for average foot; increase angle for broad foot or decrease angle for narrow foot.
7. Length of **H K** is about 1/3 or length **A B**.
8. Cut out pattern. (Fold paper on line **L M**, so both sides will be symmetrical.)
9. See general instructions items 12-15.
10. Fold leather inside out.
11. Bring **H** and **H'** together. Use whip stitch with 1/8" spacing. (See Fig. 2)
12. Sew from **H** to **K**.
13. Gather toe flap (center point) to **K** and **K'**.
14. Use 1/8" spacing on **K** side, but use 1/4" spacing of curve of flap as it must be "gathered" to the **K** side. Tie off all thread and endings.
15. Return to **K'** and repeat spacing to complete toe.
16. Cut out "tongue insert". Place it on moccasin at the center point of **H H'**. (See Fig. 2)
17. Repeat spacing--1/8" on tongue insert and 1/4" spacing on side pieces as they must be gathered.
18. Sew both sides the same till the "foot opening" equals 1/2 the length of the moccasin.
19. Bring heel point **X X'** together and sew down the heel cut. (See page 17)
20. Turn moccasin out-side-out. Notch the heel tab.
21. Extensions can be added around foot opening if desired. This piece will be foot length plus 4 inches; the height can vary, but a "wrap around top" will be 5 to 6 inches in width.
22. Sew extensions by allowing 2" flap at the tongue seam. (See Fig. 4-a, page 15)
23. Tie string is attached at 4 to 6 places around the moccasin. (See Fig. 3) All tie holes are made by a round awl such as an ice pick. They are never cut.
24. Length of tie strings are about 36" for a "wrap-around top".
25. Strings are made from scrap. (See Fig. 5, page 15.)

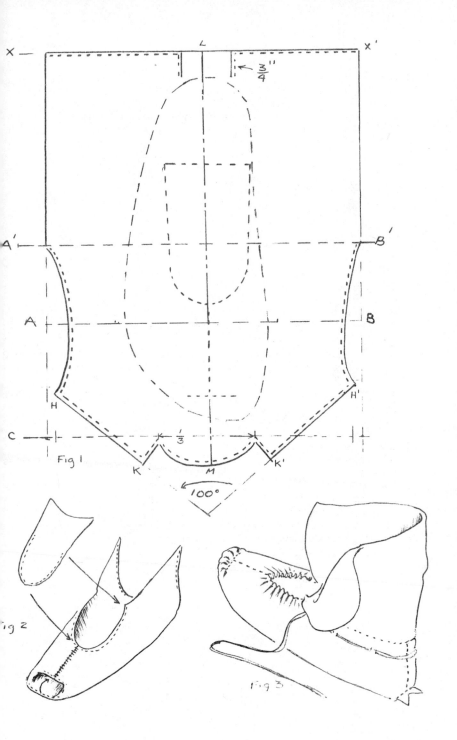

X — L X'

← ¾"

A' B'

A B

H H'

C ⅓

Fig 1 K M K'

100°

Fig 2

Fig 3

-27-

GILJAK SAKHALIN

1. See General Instructions.
2. **A B** is circumference of the foot.
3. **A' B'** is about 3/4" to 1" less than **A B**.
4. **L M** is measured by allowing 1 1/2" at heel, or measure up the heel about 2", then to the big toe and to middle of the big toe nail. See general instructions, Fig. G-3.
5. **J J'** is 1/2 circumference plus 1/2" or measure on line **A B**, under foot and up on each side level of top of foot.
6. Mark **J J'** measure on tracing. This will give **J K** and **M** base line.
7. Point **K** on line **J K** is 1/2 the distance from toe on tracing and **M** - the length of is 1/4 of **L M** starting at intersection of **J K** and **M** base line.
8. **H K** is slightly longer than **J K**.
9. The triangular "insert" is Fig. 16.
10. SEWING: This moccasin is sewn right side out as the leather is heavy and seams are larger. So for comfort the seam will be outside.
11. Bring **H** to **H'**. Use a whip stitch or (double glover or harness stitch). Sew from **H** to **K**.
12. Bring point **M** to **K K'**. Gather leather from point **M** to **J** to line **J K** by using 1/2" stitch on **J K** and 1/4" stitch to curve **M J**.
13. After toe is sewn turn to heel. Join **X X'** and sew to **Y'**. Bring **L** point to **Y** and sew.
14. Sew in triangular piece and measure "foot opening". This determines the length of top pieces.
15. The boot top can vary in height. 8" is a good width which added to the moccasin height will give 10" to 11" overall height. If the tops are one piece the seam will be in the back. If two pieces the second seam will be in front. If three pieces the third seam will be on the side. If four pieces, seams front- back-both sides.

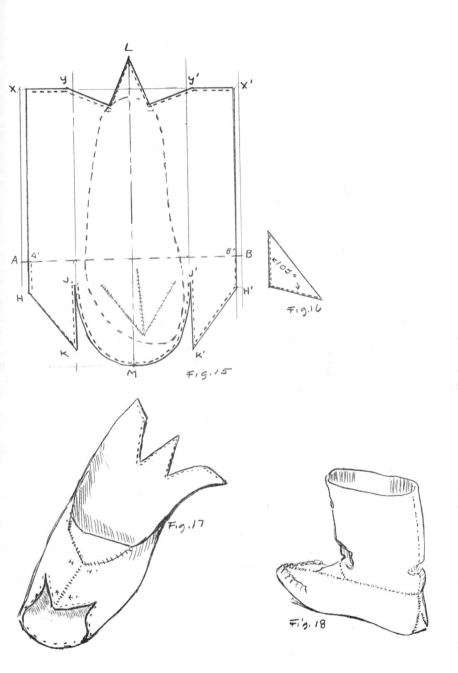

Fig. 15

Fig. 16

Fig. 17

Fig. 18

ONEIDA - IROQUOIAN

1. See General Instructions.
2. **A B** is full circumference.
3. **L M** is about 1 1/4" longer than foot tracing. (This is for a foot length of 9" to 12")
   Side flaps can vary from 1 to 3 inches in width.
4. Notice that the layout is similar to that of a "side seam". The leather requirement is
   exactly the same as side seam, only the sewing varies.
5. Cut two identical pieces of leather from one pattern.
6. Fold leather inside out on **L M** ; sew from **M** to **A B**.
7. Leave foot opening large (more than 1/2 the length of moccasin)
8. Sew **X X'** to **L**.
9. See heel detail on page 17 for sewing heel.
10. Turn moccasin outside out and cut heel.

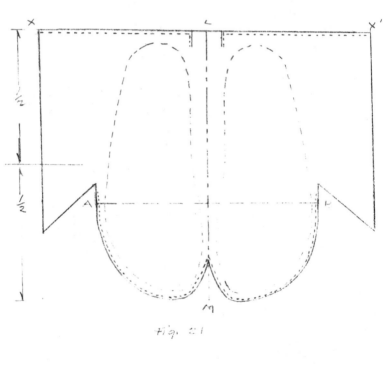

Fig. 21

SMALL "INSERT" - POINTED HEEL

See General Instructions.

A B = circumference of foot.

A'B' + insert = A B (Fig. 24)

L M is length of leather from heel to base of big toe nail. See Fig. G-3, page 13.

Sew inside out if the leather is light weight. Sew outside out if leather is heavy.

Place insert M on sole M. Use 1/8" stitch on insert piece and use 1/4" stitch on sole piece.

Sew from M to point beyond A or B.

8. The foot opening remaining should be 1/2 the length of finished moccasin.

9. If the moccasin is inside out, bring X and X' together and sew from X X' to L.

0. Turn moccasin outside out.

1. This heel is pointed as shown in Fig. 25.

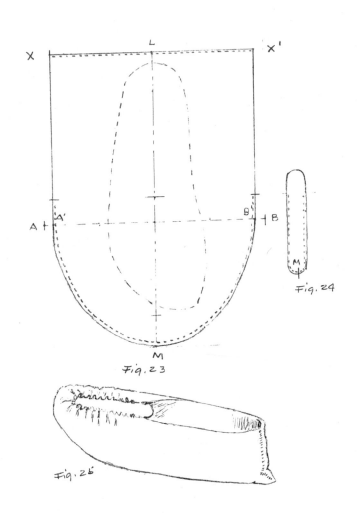

Fig. 23

Fig. 24

Fig. 25

MEDIUM INSERT - TONGUE
SQUARE HEEL

1. See General Instructions.
2. **A B** = circumference of foot.
3. **A'B'** + insert (Fig. 24) = **A B**.
4. **L M** is length of leather from heel to base of big toe nail. See Fig. G-3, page 13.
5. Sew inside out if the leather is light weight. Sew outside out if leather is heavy.
6. Place insert **M** on sole **M**. Use 1/8" stitch on insert piece and use 1/4" stitch on sole piece.
7. Sew from **M** to point beyond **A** or **B**.
8. The foot opening remaining should be 1/2 the length of finished moccasin.
9. If the moccasin is inside out, bring **X** and **X'** together and sew from **X X'** to **L**.
10. Turn moccasin outside out.
11. This heel is square with a heel tab. See heel details on page 17.

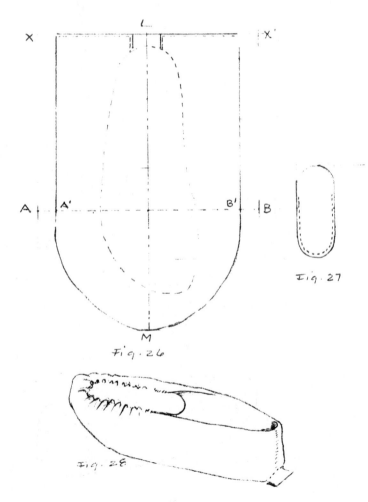

Fig. 26

Fig. 27

Fig. 28

FULL INSERT TONGUE - NO HEEL TAB

1. See General Instructions.
2. **A B** = circumference of foot.
3. **A'B'** + insert = **A B** (Fig. 24)
4. **L M** is length of leather from heel to base of big toe nail. See Fig. G-3, page 13.
5. Sew inside out if the leather is light weight. Sew outside out if leather is heavy.
6. Place insert **M** on sole **M**. Use 1/8" stitch on insert piece and use 1/4" stitch on sole piece.
7. Sew from **M** to point beyond **A** or **B**.
8. The foot opening remaining should be 1/2 the length of finished moccasin.
9. If the moccasin is inside out, bring **X** and **X'** together and sew from **X X'** to **L**.
10. Turn moccasin outside out.
11. Heel seam is a "T" seam. Note heel tab has been cut off. See heel details on page 17.

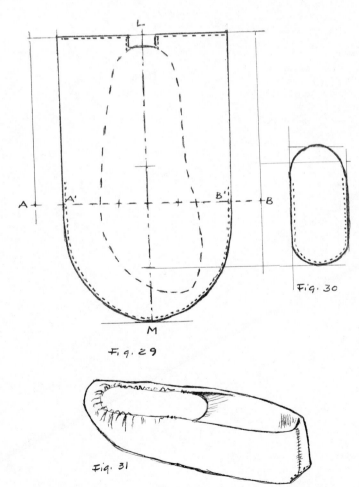

Fig. 29

Fig. 30

Fig. 31

GATHERED TOE
YUKON GATHER TOE (WRAP AROUND)

1. See general instructions.
2. **A B** = circumference
3. **A'B'** + insert tongue = **A B** (Fig.33).
4. **L M** is leather length with allowance at heel (1/2" to 3/4") under foot to base of big toe nail. (See Fig. G-3, page 13)
5. This moccasin is suited to heavy leather such as moose or elk. Heavy leather usually means wider spacing in stitches.
6. Bring insert **M** to sole **M** and sew to point beyond **A** or **B**. Use wider stitch but keep a 2 to 1 ratio, so as to "gather" the sole piece to the insert.
7. The foot opening is a bit larger for this pattern. (More than 1/2 the length of moccasin).
8. Heel is sewn from **X X'** to **L**.
9. The heel tab is tacked with a few stitches on out side. See heel details on page 17.
10. Wrap around tops are most always folder to outside.
11. The length of tops is usually determined by adding 5" to 6" to length of moccasin. Height of tops can be 6" to 8".
12. Sew on tops same as Fig. 4-a, page 15.
13. Be sure to tie off or bind the beginning and ending stitch on all tops as they receive strain at this point.
14. This pattern has no left or right foot, except by wearing.
15. Note the position of tie strings. Strings are cut (See Fig. 5, page 15) from scrap and are about 36" long.
16. Holes for tie-strings are forced open with an awl or pointed tool. They are never cut.

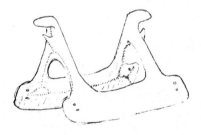

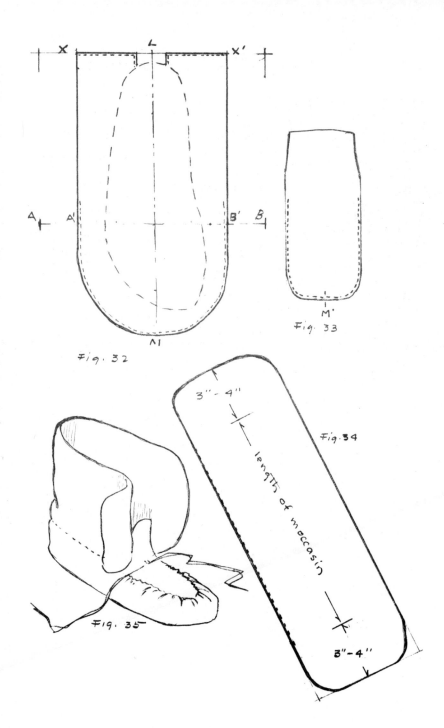

X   L   X'

A ⊢ A'   B'   B

A1

Fig. 32

M'

Fig. 33

Fig. 34

3" - 4"

length of moccasin

3" - 4"

Fig. 35

YUKON BOOT TOP

1. See General Instructions.
2. **A B** = circumference.
3. **A'B'** + insert-tongue = **A B** (Fig. 37).
4. **L M** is leather length with allowance at heel (1/2" to 3/4") under foot to base of big toe nail. (See Fig. G-3, page 13).
5. This moccasin is suited to heavy leather such as moose or elk. Heavy leather usually means wider spacing in stitching.
6. Attach "insert tongue" to sole and sew to point **A** or **B**. Use wider stitch but keep a 2 to 1 ratio so as to "gather" the sole piece to the insert.
7. The foot opening is a bit larger for this pattern. (More than 1/2 the length of moccasin.)
8. Heel is sewn from **X X'** to **L**.
9. The heel tab is tacked with a few stitches on outside. See heel details on page 17.
10. See Fig. 39 and 38. The boot top may be 8". The length or circumference can be found by careful measuring of foot opening.
11. Start at heel seam (See Fig. 38) and sew around foot opening, then up the back.
12. This is a bit difficult sewing, but it can be done and the resulting seam will be inside.
13. Note location of tie string on this pattern. This being a snow moccasin has few holds as possible. See general instructions for making holes for ties.

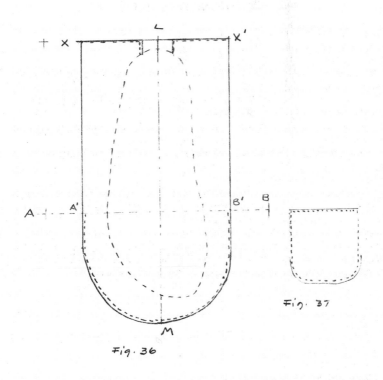

Fig. 36

Fig. 37

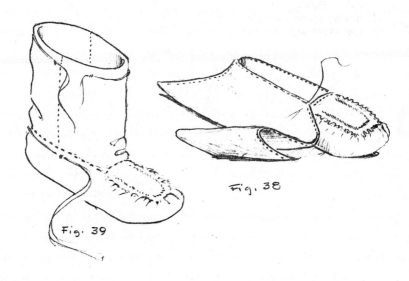

Fig. 38

Fig. 39

MUKLUK
GATHERED TOE AND HEEL - "SHAPED SOLE"

1. See General Instructions.
2. Determine **A' B'** by measuring foot (at line **A B**) about 3/4" above line.
3. **A'B'** plus vamp (See Fig. 42) must equal circumference. Note that line **A'B'** is point to measure and that points **Y** and **Z** are midway or 1/2 length of shaped sole. Add 1/2" to **A B** measurement as this is loose fitting.
4. The curve **A' MB'** is just slightly smaller than the foot outline around the toes. If the curve is made symmetrically the pattern may be used for both Mukluk. See Fig. 42.
5. The "gathering" at toe and heel must pull the leather in to foot size.
6. The best "gathering" is done by dampening the toe and heel. Be sure not to get it too damp or the leather will swell and make the gathering more difficult.
7. Use a strong nylon or linen thread and by as small a stitch as possible, 1/8" weave the thread in and out, such as in Fig. 57 on page 42.
8. Tie off one end of the thread and work in the creases or folds. Work the folds several times if need be before tying off thread. Do the same with the heel. Work the folds at both toe and heels till the right size is obtained, then tie off both draw threads.
9. Center vamp piece (See Fig. 42) over shaped sole. See if points **Y** and **Z** reach the midpoint on shaped sole piece. If the tow pieces match, start sewing.
10. Start sewing at point **M** (outside out) catch every fold with a "whip stitch". See stitch sheet, pages 18 and 19. Sew to point **Y** or **Z** and tie off. Start at **M** again and sew other side.
11. The boot tops are sewn on next. Measure from **Z** to around heel to **Y**. This gives length of top piece. See Fig. 42. (Note that **K Y** and **K Z** are same length as shown in Fig.42 as **Z L**. **Z L Y** on Fig. 43 must be same length as sole from **Z L Y**.
12. Sew front first from **K** to **Z**, then **K** to **Y**. (See Fig. 44) Sew from **Z** to **Y** around the heel. (Outside out).
13. Be sure to sew in tie strips. These slope to the rear as they cross around the heel and tie in front at the ankle.

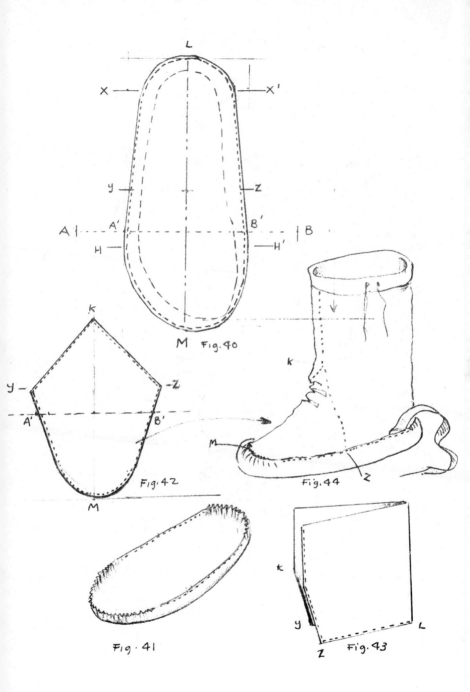

L

X —————— X'

y   z

A | A' ———————— B' | B

H ———————— H'

M Fig. 40

k

y —   — z

A'   B'

M Fig. 42

Fig. 41

k

y

z   Fig. 43   L

k

M

Fig. 44   z

1. See General Instructions.
2. **A B** = circumference of foot.
3. **A' B'** = width of sole leather.
4. **L M** = length of sole piece.
5. **A' B'** and **L M** measurements should be 3/4" to 1" above floor line.
6. Two sole pieces will be made--one for the right foot and one for the left. Cut from similar leather.
7. Two vamp-tops are cut for left and right. See Fig. 45 - solid line.
8. The sole pieces are moistened to aid in shaping. A draw string can be used as with the other "shaped soles". See Fig. 41 on page 39 and 57 on page 47.
9. **C'** (on both foot outlines) marks end of sewing from **M** to **C'**. **C'** to **C** is sewn later as sewing is completed. From **M D** - and **D X** around the sole. **X** is joined to point **C'** under **Y** flap.
10. Sewing is done outside out and can be done in the usual manner or laced by pre-punching the hole in sole and vamp pieces. This method requires considerable attention to spacing of holes as the sole must be "gathered".

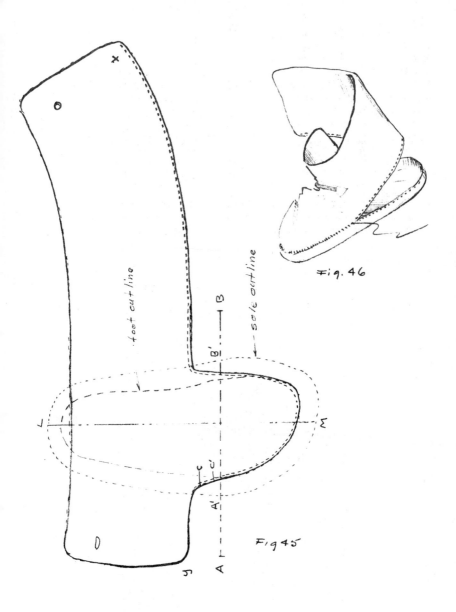

foot cutline

sole outline

Fig. 46

Fig 45

APACHE SHAPED-SOLE 3 - PIECE

1. See General Instructions.
2. **A B** = circumference.
3. **A'B'** + vamp = **A B**.
4. Note vamp widens at points **J** and **K**, also that **J** and **K** extend beyond mid-point.
5. Note that **J'** and **K'** overlap point **J** and **K**. The overlap is about 1".
6. The sole piece is about 3/4" wider than foot tracing.
7. The vamp is same size as foot tracing over toe but becomes wider at points **J** and **K**.
   A' B' should fit snugly but loosely at points **J** and **K**.
8. Cut 2 sole pieces, be sure to turn the pattern over for second sole.
9. Cut 2 vamp pieces, be sure to turn the pattern for second vamp.
10. Cut 2 back pieces. (See Fig. 48. Note the shape of the ends.)
11. Shape sole by using draw string as shown in Fig. 57, page 47.
12. The shaped sole should fit the foot.
13. Sew from **M** to **J**, or **K**. Be sure to secure the gathered sole to the vamp piece.
14. Start sewing back piece at **J'** overlapping **J** about 1". Sew around heel to point
    K'. If **K'** point is too long it can be trimmed before completing the sewing.
15. The tie string is about 16" long.

Geronimo
ıld Photos

Barboncito

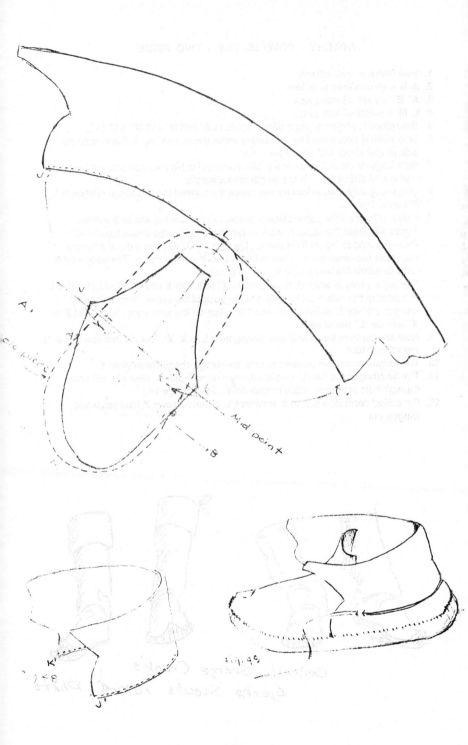

APACHE - POINTED TOE - TWO PIECE

1. See General Instructions.
2. **A B** = circumference of foot.
3. **A' B'** = width of sole piece.
4. **L M'** = length of sole piece.
5. Sole piece is shown as outer dotted line **L** to **A'** and **M'** and **M'** to **B'** to **L**.
6. Sole width is determined by measuring under the foot on line **A B** and upon the side of foot about 1/2" above floor line.
7. Sole length is measured on line **L M'**: from heel to big toe, add same at heel as at side and add at toe, 1/4 the length of foot length.
8. In drawing sole around foot tracing notice the pointed toe position in relation to **L M** center line.
9. Figure 50 shows the upper piece in respect to foot tracing and sole outline. Figure 52 shows the upper in more detail. Note the wedge shape insert which is where the tongue Figure 51 is sewn. <u>Caution</u> : DO NOT make this cut till sole and upper has been sewn. Then cut from **L** to **Y** can be made. The wedge cut is made to adjust the vamp over instep for proper fit.
10. The upper piece is sewn from toe point to **X'** or **X** with **X** and **X'** meeting to point **L**.
11. The point of the sole must be drawn to the point of the upper. This is done by using a 1/8" stitch on the upper and 1/4" stitch on the sole piece, until point **X** or **X'** falls on "**L**" line at heel.
12. After sewing from toe to heel and sewing from **L** to **X X'**, cut the foot opening to fit the arch of foot.
13. The tongue-insert can be sewn in to fill the wedge shape below point **Y**
14. The tie string about 14-16" long is attached on both sides, (See Fig. 53) and through hole in tongue. (See tongue detail sheet, page 16.)
15. For added decoration a 2" to 3" wide welt strip can be sewn in heel seam and fringes cut.

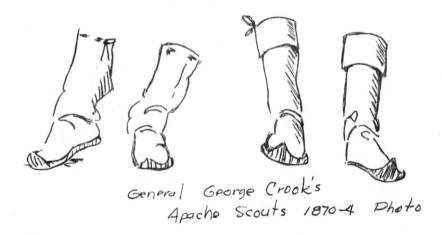

General George Crook's
Apache Scouts 1870-4 Photo

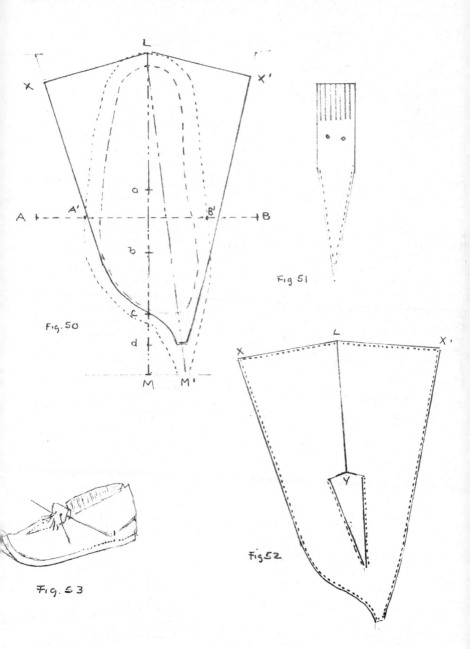

Fig. 50

Fig 51

Fig 52

Fig. 53

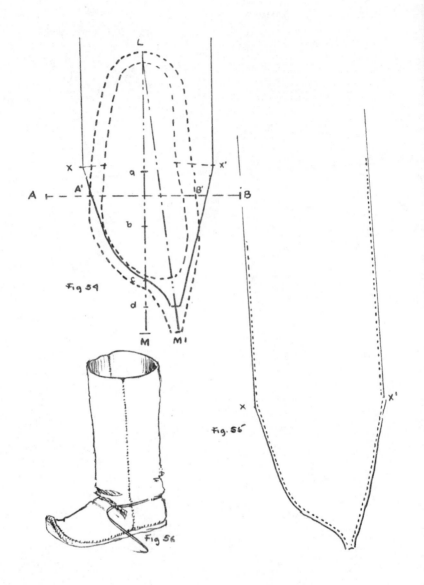

Fig 54

Fig. 55

Fig 56

SIMPLE "PUCKER" SLIPPER TYPE

1. Trace foot on paper. See general instructions.
2. **A' B'** is 1/2" to 1" less than **A B**.
3. **L M** is foot length (tracing) plus 1/2" at heel, plus 2" to 2 1/2" at toe, or measure from heel over big toe to joint of big toe (base). See Fig. G-3, page 13.
4. Connect **A'M** and **B'M** with a gentle curve.
5. Fold pattern on line **L M** as this can be symmetrical. There is no left or right.
6. Trace two patterns on leather (See leather instructions on page 14.)
7. With an awl make holes about 1/4 to 3/8 inches apart and use a heavy strong thread; lace in and out. (See Fig. 57.)
8. Draw up thread, as in Fig. 58, as tightly as possible. Tie the two ends of thread with a good knot.
9. Sew heel by joining **X X'** and sew down to **L**. (This produces a pointed heel.) Tie off thread.
10. Make second moccasin in same manner.

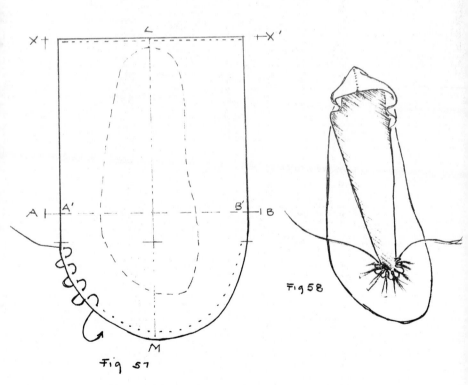

Fig 57

Fig 58

SALISH (FLATHEAD) SIDE SEAM

1. See General Instructions.
2. Make foot tracing.
3. Measure **A B** (allow 1/4" for seam) See Fig. 59.
4. Fold paper on line **L M** so that **A** and **B** come together, and foot tracing is located as shown in Fig. 59.
5. Allow about 3/4" at heel and 1/2" at toe at line **L M**. (This measurement is for average foot of 9" to 12" long and medium weight leather.)
6. Cut folded paper from **L** through points **M** to **M'**.
7. This pattern is for either left or right foot.
8. Trace pattern of leather. (See general instructions.)
9. Cut leather.
10. Foot tracing can be cut now or later. Caution: Be sure to cut opening so that there is a left and right moccasin, and that grain or flesh sides of leather are matched.
11. The foot opening **L'** to **J K** line (See Fig. 59) is 1/2 the length of **L M**. **J K** is about 2" long.
12. Note dotted tongue position is wider than **J K**. This gives a tuck-in tip as shown in tongue detail sheet on page 16.
13. The tongue, Fig. 60, can be made of scrap or flank leather, about 2 1/2" wide and 6 to 8 " long.
14. Fold both pieces of leather grain side in. Start sewing at **M'** and around to **X X'**. Be sure to check points **X** and **X'** occasionally during sewing to see that they match. Some sewing produces a "creeping" of the leather and as a result the points **X** and **X'** do not end up even.
15. Tie off thread at point **X X'** and if foot opening has been cut, start at **L'** and sew to within 3/4" of bottom. See heel detail sheet, page 17.
16. Sew heel and tab before turning inside out.
17. Sew on tongue. Lay tongue grain side down on vamp and bring edge to line **J K** and sew. See tongue detail, page 17.
18. The tops or extensions are usually 6" wide or higher and are 5" to 6" longer than the length of **L M** or length of moccasin.
19. Note Fig. 4-a, page 15. The long side of top flap fold over the other short side from the inside to outside.
20. Lay top piece against the foot opening (See Fig. 4-a) grain side down.
21. Tie both ends of this seam securely.
22. Tie strings can be attached next. See tongue detail U, page 16.
23. Make strings at least 36" long. See Fig. 5, page 15.

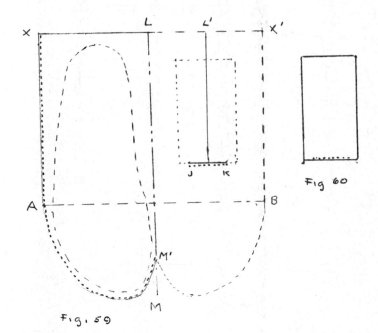

X   L   L'   X'

J   K

A   B

M'

M

Fig. 59

Fig 60

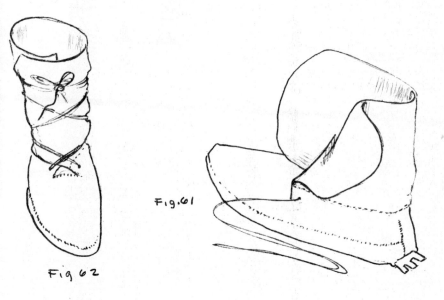

Fig. 61

Fig 62

-49-

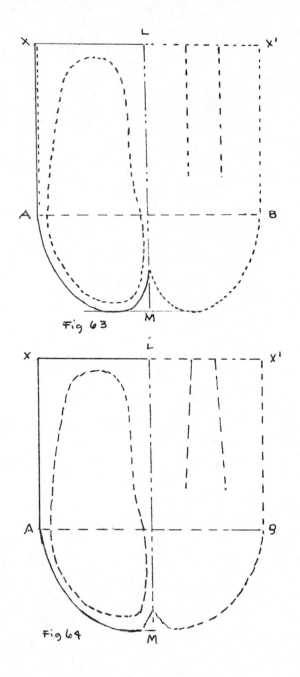

Fig 63

Fig 64

Flathead Dancers

PAIUTE - SHAPED SOLE - TWO PIECE

1. See General Instructions.
2. **A B** = circumference of foot. (Fig.65)
3. **A'B'** = width of sole piece which is measured under foot and up on side of foot about 3/4" above floor line.
4. The vamp or upper piece at line **A B** is wider than usual. Note this on pattern. The tie string is located to draw the foot opening closed.
5. Note the two lines from Point **X** to toes and **X'** to toe. The outside lines will make the back high - if so desired - the inner line will lower the height of the back.
6. Cut two upper pieces, one for each foot.
7. The easiest way to shape the sole is to put a draw string around toes and heel. See Fig. 57. Draw toe and heel in until sole is size of foot tracing or fits the foot itself.
9. After shaping soles, sew from **M** to heel. Use a whip stitch and tie the "gathers" of the sole to the vamp.
10. Do not make tie string holes till after sewing and putting on foot.
11. This same design can be used with a flat parfleche sole by adjusting measurements.

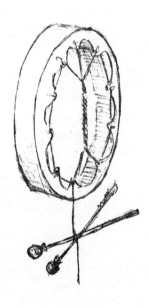

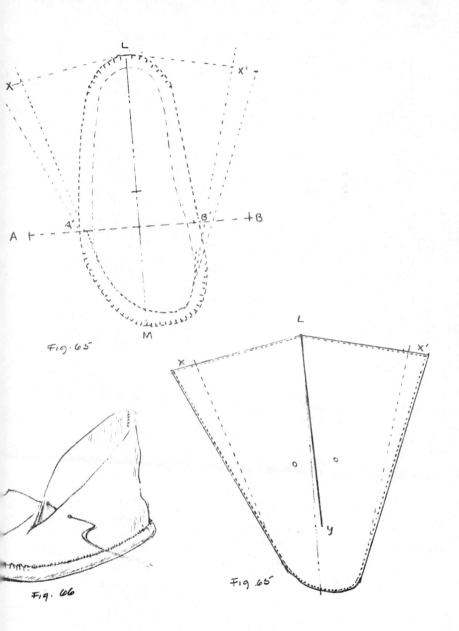

Fig. 65

Fig. 66

Fig. 65

KIOWA APACHE

1. See General Instructions.
2. This design is for a hard sole, but a soft sole could be used.
3. The sole piece is about 1/4" longer than foot tracing.
4. The vamp - upper piece - at points **A B** is wider than the sole. When added to sole will be equal to **A B**. Allow 1/4" for seams.
5. The vamp - upper extends 2 1/2" to 3" beyond the **L** point.
6. Sew toe to heel and as a precaution do not cut fringe at heel seam until the heel is sewn.
7. Sew heel with a double glover's stitch or harness stitch.
8. Note the upper flap is not sewn.
9. Fig. 76 shows the tongue which is sewn on **J'K'** line to the foot opening **J K**. Fold the tongue on **J'K'** over **J K** with the square piece up. Use a whip stitch to catch the 3 thicknesses of leather.
10. After sewing pull the square end upright, and put holes in the fringed side of tongue. See Fig. 77.
11. The tie-string is about 16" long.

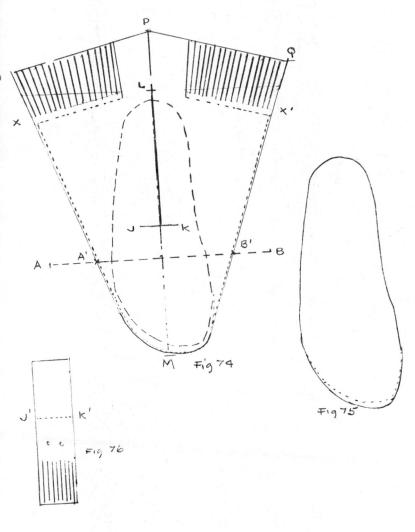

P

Q

X   X'

L

J   k

A   A'   B'   B

M   Fig 74

J'   k'   Fig 76

Fig 75

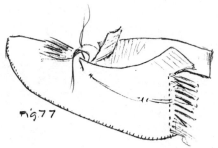

Fig 77

WINNEBAGO CENTER SEAM

1. See General Instructions.
2. See Fig. 59, on page 49, for the pattern of side seam style moccasin. Pattern and layout are the same as this center seam.
3. Place foot tracing on extra large pattern. See G-1, page 12.
4. Note placement of foot tracing. Fig. 78.
5. **AB**, **XX'** and **M** are identical to side seam layout.
6. The flap **X' B2 A2** to **X** is about 1" longer than **L M** length.
7. **J X** and **KX'** may vary in length but 3 inches is a good length.
8. **A2 B2** will never be longer than **A'B'**.
9. **L'M'** of the flap is center line of flap which falls on **L M** line, after flap is sewn to foot opening.
10. **L'M'** can vary in length. A good length is 1/2 length of foot tracing.
11. Cut pattern on outside line and cut heel. Do not cut the dotted line.
12. Trace pattern on leather, see G-4, page 14, close to edge of leather. Check leather under pattern for cuts, thin spots or holes.
13. Turn pattern over for second tracing so there will be a left and right moccasin.
14. Fold leather along line **L M**. Sew around t point **L' N**. Fold flap around. Bring **X'** of flap to **X'** at heel. Sew from **L' N** to **X'**.
15. Bring **X** and **X'** together, insert 16 X 1/2 inch tie string and sew it at **X X'** point. Sew down to heel cut. See heel detail sheet.
16. Sew across the heel. See Fig. 79.
17. The front flap may be worn turned up or turned down.

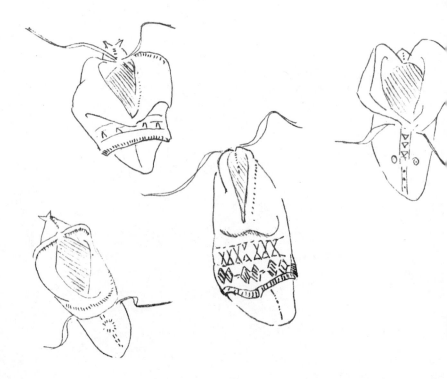

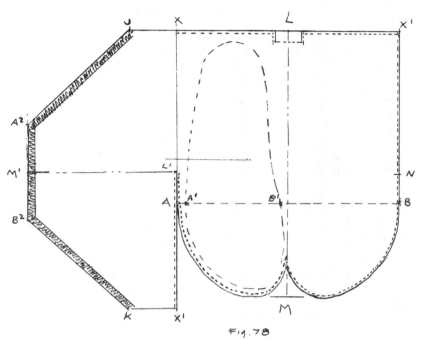

Fig. 78

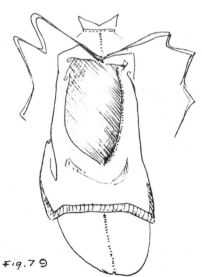

Fig. 79

ASSINIBOINE - HARD SOLE OR SOFT SOLE

1. This design is two pieces; a sole piece and an upper piece. The sole can be made of different leather, such as heavier or half tanned rawhide, or of the same material as uppers.
2. See general instructions.
3. Note **A B + A'B'** = circumference + 1/4" for seams.
4. Make usual foot tracings. (See general instructions.) Make second tracing for sole pattern.
5. **L M** on this pattern is foot measurement + 1/2" at heel and 1/2" at toe, because line **M X** is a bit long on this pattern. Draw pattern of foot tracing and cut out.
6. Trace pattern (see general instructions) on leather. Be sure to turn the pattern over for second tracing as this design has a left and right foot. Cut foot opening **L** to **J K** and cut **J K**.
7. Start sewing by placing leather with the upper centered on line **L M** but even with sole piece. Start at **M** and sew to **X** at heel. Return to **M** and sew second side to **X'**.
8. The tongue is attached and tie string holes are made with an awl. See general instructions. A 12" to 16" tie string is needed. Tops or fringe may be added. Measure around foot opening and cut a strip of leather about one inch longer than this measurement and about 2 1/2 to 3 " wide. Lay this strip inside even with the tongue piece and use a whip stitch.. Sew around to opposite tongue piece. (Be sure to place flesh side to flesh side) When finished the top is folded over outside or pulled up and fringes cut.

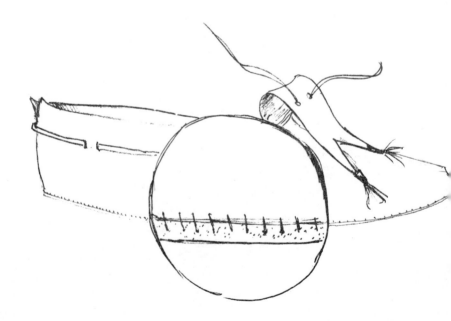

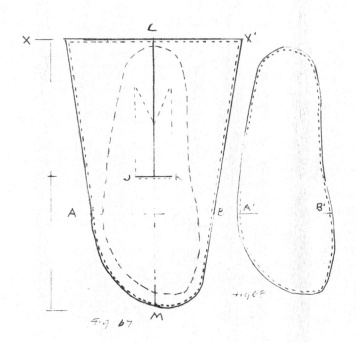

Fig 67

Fig 68

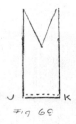

Fig 69

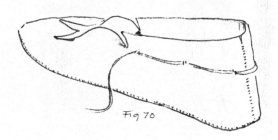

Fig 70

UTE TYPE - HARD SOLE

1. See General Instructions.
2. Note in particular - conditions along line **A B**. The dotted foot outline and points **A'B'** of the vamp-upper piece are more than circumference of **A B**. This makes the moccasin a bit loose over arch. This is desirable with a hard sole.
3. Note also **X** and **X'** are dropped down form the horizontal line. This is because the distance from **A'** to **L** must equal distance from **A'** to **X**.
4. The tongue can be cut before sewing, cut from **L** to **J** and **L** to **K**. Distance between **J** and **K** will be about 2".
5. This particular tongue design is often found in baby moccasins, as there is no harsh seam to bite into the baby's foot.
6. The sole, if hard sole, will be about 1/4" longer than foot outline.
7. Sew from **M** to heel. Take a bit wider stitch in vamp piece than sole and the vamp a greater distance around the toe.
8. Sew up on heel seam. Start at sole seam if the leather varies and end up uneven at top; it can be trimmed.
9. The tie string is about 16" long.
10. Tops may be added if desired. See Fig. 4-b.

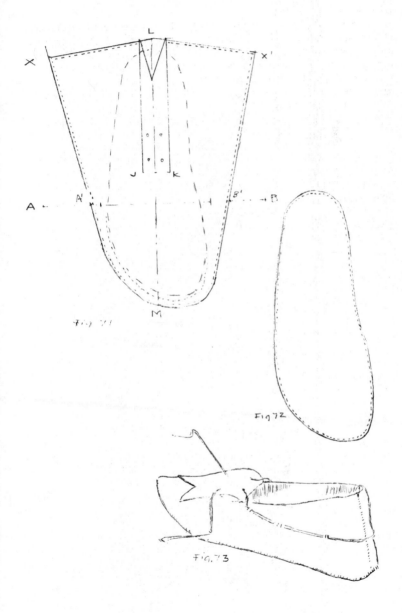

X

X'

L

J K

A A' B' B

M

Fig 71

Fig 72

Fig. 73

CHITIMACHA CENTER SEAM

1. See General Instructions.
2. **A B** = circumference. (Fig. 80).
3. **L M** = usual length of leather. (3/4" at heel and 1/2" at toe)
4. **L M'** is length needed for this pattern.,
5. **M'** is found by measuring under foot, 3/4" at heel, under big toe and up to middle of toe nail. See Fig. G-3, page 13.
6. Distance between points **J** and **J'** is measured under foot and up on each side 1/4" about top of foot. See Fig. G-6, page 14.
7. Distance between **H** and **H'** is greater than **A B** at midpoint of moccasin length.
8. To find the arc of **J M'** and **J'** establish the three points and make a circular sketch as shown. Fig. 80.
9. The circular flap will be gathered over toe as shown in Fig. 81.
10. The top flap **H** to **X** can be a free form sweep, or if a higher top is desired make top along dotted line. This applies to **H' X'** as well.
11. Sew heel from **L** heel cut to top of back seam.
12. In sewing, this is design is for heavy leather and all seams are on the outside.
13. Bring **H** and **H'** together. Use a bold whip stitch. Sew **K** to **K'**.
14. Bring **M'** to **K K'** point and sew to **J** or **J'**. Use at least 1/4" stitch in toe flap, and 1/8" stitch along **J K** line. This will gather the toe flap enough to produce the "pucker". Sew the other half the same way.
15. The heel can be sewn next and the heel tab finished in several ways. See heel details, page 17.
16. Cut tie string about 24" long. (See Fig. 5)
17. Attach tie string as shown in Fig. 81. Note the long flap is on inside and folds to outside of foot.
18. There is no left or right except for the length of top flap.

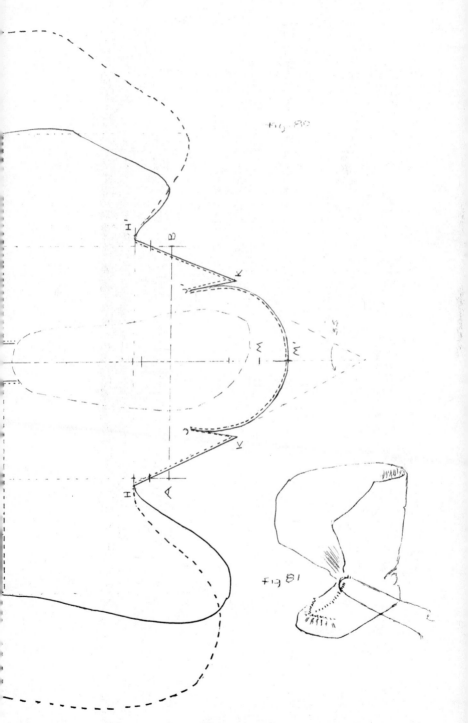

Fig. 80

Fig. 81

-63-

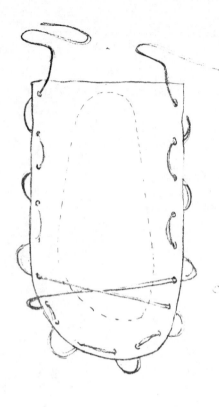

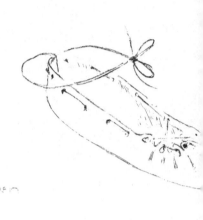

open

Promontory
(900 yr. old
slipper)

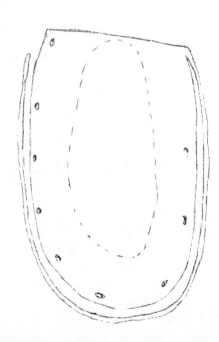

Dew-claw- (Hog-up)
& other places -
u+sl)

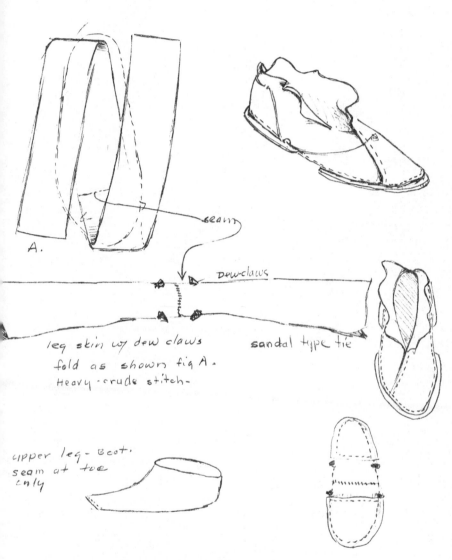

seam

A.

Dew-claws

leg skin w/ dew claws
fold as shown fig A.
Heavy-crude stitch-

sandal type tie

upper leg - Boot.
seam at toe
only

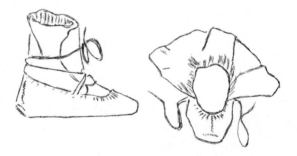

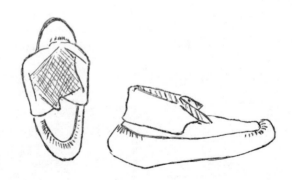

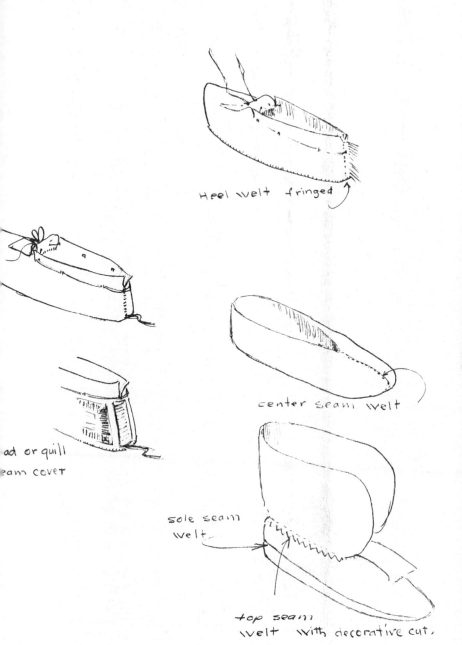

Heel welt fringed

center seam welt

ad or quill
eam cover

sole seam
welt

top seam
welt with decorative cut.

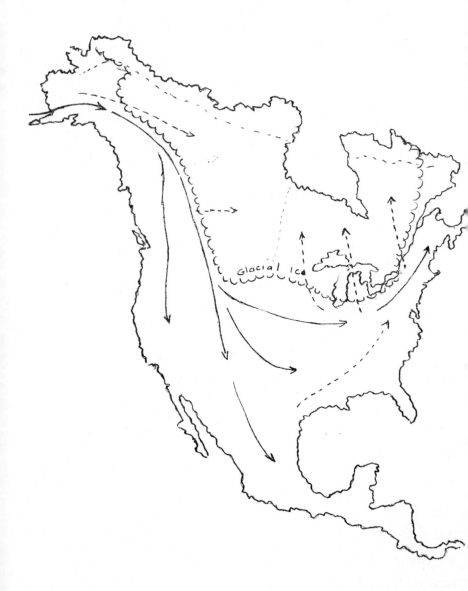

Glacial Ice

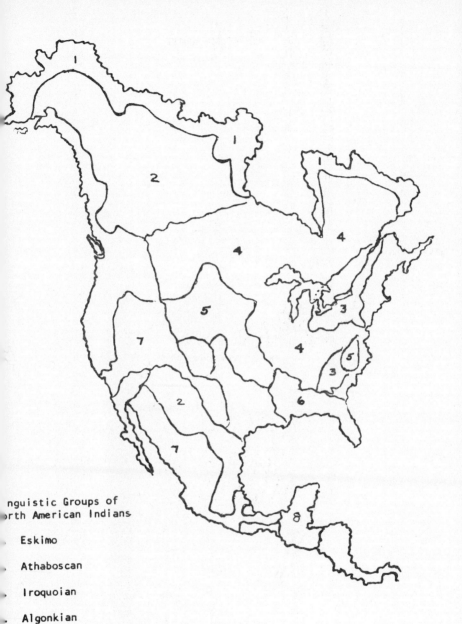

Linguistic Groups of
North American Indians

. Eskimo

. Athaboscan

. Iroquoian

. Algonkian

. Siouan

. Muskogean

. Uto-Aztecan

. Mayan

Navajo

Navajo 1893 Photo